The earliest dinosaurs were little meat-eaters, like *Chindesaurus* (CHIN-dee-SAW-rus). It lived in the Late Triassic Period. *Chindesaurus* had to be careful. Giant meat-eaters like *Smilosuchus* (SMY-luh-SOOK-us), a relative of crocodiles, liked to eat these small early dinosaurs.

Smilosuchus lived in lakes and rivers. Another giant crocodile relative, *Poposaurus* (POH-poh-SAW-rus), chased *Chindesaurus* on land. But the early dinosaurs survived! And some grew bigger and BIGGER!

YOU ARE HERE

TRIASSIC	JURASSIC	CRETACEOUS	AGE OF MAMMALS

250   200   145   65   NOW
MILLIONS OF YEARS AGO

Many dinosaurs became huge—bigger than elephants—
in the Jurassic Period! *Stegosaurus* (STEG-uh-SAW-rus) lived
in the Late Jurassic. It was a plant-eater with armor plates
sticking out of its back and sharp spikes on its tail.

YOU ARE HERE

| TRIASSIC | JURASSIC | CRETACEOUS | AGE OF MAMMALS |

250 200 145 65 NOW
MILLIONS OF YEARS AGO

Stegosaurus fought a big Jurassic meat-eater called *Allosaurus* (AL-uh-SAW-rus). We dug up an *Allosaurus* skeleton that had a hole in its hipbone. The hole fit the tail spike of a stegosaur. So we know the stegosaur had scored a direct hit.

Many giant long-necked dinosaurs lived in the Late Jurassic Period. We dug up the footprints of a baby *Apatosaurus* (uh-PAT-uh-SAW-rus). Danger was nearby! Close to the baby's tracks we found tracks from a huge meat-eater, *Torvosaurus* (TOR-vuh-SAW-rus).

YOU ARE HERE

TRIASSIC	JURASSIC	CRETACEOUS	AGE OF MAMMALS
250 200	145	65	NOW

MILLIONS OF YEARS AGO

But the baby *Apatosaurus* was safe. Right next to its tracks were the footprints of an adult *Apatosaurus*, probably its mother or father. An adult *Apatosaurus* fought with its long, whiplike tail. The tail was 30 feet long—as long as a school bus!

Fossil teeth tell us that meat-eaters worked hard to
raise their babies. Dinosaurs lost teeth when they fed. And then
they grew new ones. They grew new teeth all through their lives.
Crocodiles do that today.

We dug up the bones of a *Brachiosaurus* (BRACK-ee-uh-SAW-rus),
a Late Jurassic plant-eater. And mixed in with the bones, we found
teeth from an adult and a baby *Ceratosaurus* (suh-RAT-uh-SAW-rus)—
a meat-eater. That means the ceratosaur adult and baby ate together—
just like a mom lion does with her cubs.

YOU ARE HERE

TRIASSIC   JURASSIC   CRETACEOUS   AGE OF MAMMALS

250   200   145   65   NOW
MILLIONS OF YEARS AGO

During the Cretaceous Period, some dinosaurs became very fast and very smart. *Deinonychus* (dy-NON-ih-kus) was a meat-eater that lived in the Early Cretaceous. It was only as heavy as a big dog.

But *Deinonychus* was speedy and had a big brain. Packs of *Deinonychus* attacked like kickboxers. They slashed with their super-sharp hind claws. That's why *Deinonychus* could kill large plant-eaters like the long-tailed *Tenontosaurus* (teh-NON-tuh-SAW-rus).

The Late Cretaceous dinosaurs grew the biggest
fins and frills. *Spinosaurus* (SPY-nuh-SAW-rus) was
a gigantic fish-eater with a sail on its back. The sail
made its body look taller and scarier.

Spinosaurs fought each other over the best fishing spots. They would huff and puff and stand on their tiptoes trying to frighten each other. Lizards with tall sails fight this way today.

YOU ARE HERE

TRIASSIC · JURASSIC · CRETACEOUS · AGE OF MAMMALS

250 200 145 65 NOW
MILLIONS OF YEARS AGO

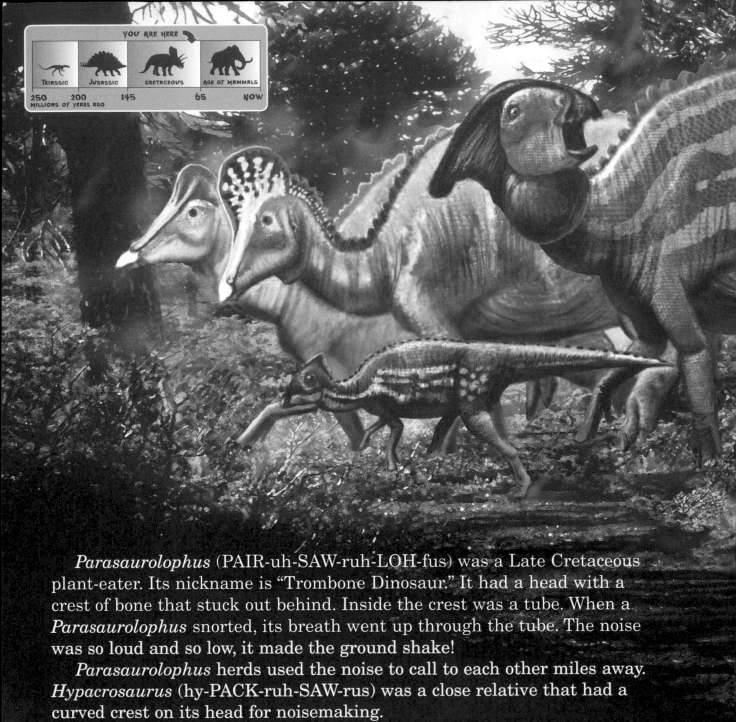

Parasaurolophus (PAIR-uh-SAW-ruh-LOH-fus) was a Late Cretaceous plant-eater. Its nickname is "Trombone Dinosaur." It had a head with a crest of bone that stuck out behind. Inside the crest was a tube. When a *Parasaurolophus* snorted, its breath went up through the tube. The noise was so loud and so low, it made the ground shake!

Parasaurolophus herds used the noise to call to each other miles away. *Hypacrosaurus* (hy-PACK-ruh-SAW-rus) was a close relative that had a curved crest on its head for noisemaking.

Torosaurus (TOR-uh-SAW-rus) was a plant-eater with long horns. It lived 66 million years ago, at the very end of the Mesozoic Era. *Torosaurus* had the biggest, strongest head of any dinosaur. Its skull was eight feet long!

Torosaurus needed its long horns and strong head to fight the meat-eater *Tyrannosaurus* (ty-RAN-uh-SAW-rus). *Tyrannosaurus* had the strongest jaws and thickest teeth of any meat-eating dinosaur. One bite could crush a hipbone or rib cage.

Plant-eaters fought each other, too. Male plant-eaters would fight to impress females. *Stygimoloch* (STIJ-ih-MOH-lock) was a plant-eater the size of a sheep. It had a built-in helmet made from bone and a thick neck like a football player. One *Stygimoloch* would try to ram another *Stygimoloch* in the stomach.

Edmontonia (ED-mun-TONE-ee-yuh) was an armored plant-eater with spikes on its shoulders. The spikes were long and sharp. One blow could kill a *Tyrannosaurus*.

Microraptor (MY-kroh-RAP-tur) was a tiny relative of *Deinonychus*. It lived in the Early Cretaceous and was no larger than a big crow. *Microraptor* had long fingers with sharp claws. It could climb trees by digging its claws into the bark.

And *Microraptor* could soar like a flying squirrel! Fossils dug in China show that *Microraptor* skin was covered in feathers, just like a bird's!

That means . . .

. . . some dinosaurs are still alive today. All birds—ostriches and hummingbirds, eagles and parrots—came from an ancestor like *Microraptor*. When you pet a parakeet, you're petting a genuine great great-GREAT-grandchild of a dinosaur!